# The Daily Debrief

WIN IN LIFE AND BUSINESS WITH THE COMBAT
PILOTS' SECRET TO HIGH PERFORMANCE

## Jeff Bonner

THE DAILY DEBRIEF. Copyright © 2019 by Jeff Bonner.

All rights reserved. No part of this publication may be reproduced, distributed or transmitted in any form or by any means, including photocopying, recording, or other electronic or mechanical methods, without the prior written permission of the publisher, except in the case of brief quotations embodied in critical reviews and certain other noncommercial uses permitted by copyright law. For permission requests, write to the publisher, addressed "Attention: Permissions Coordinator," at the following address: Dual Wings Press, Baltimore, MD 21111.

www.Daily-Debrief.com

The appearance of US Department of Defense (DoD) visual information does not imply or constitute DoD endorsement.

Ordering Information:
Quantity sales. Special discounts are available on quantity purchases by corporations, associations, and others. For details, contact the "Special Sales Department" at www.daily-debrief.com/contact.

The Daily Debrief / Jeff Bonner—1st ed.
ISBN 978-0-578-58805-6

# Contents

| | | |
|---|---|---|
| AUTHOR'S NOTE | | 08 |
| INTRODUCTION | | 11 |

## PART 1  IT'S TIME TO WIN

1. FROM THE TREADMILL TO PROSPERITY — 16

2. THE DAILY DEBRIEF ASSESSMENT — 18

## PART 2  DISCOVERING THE POWER OF THE DAILY DEBRIEF

3. DEBRIEF - MILITARY AVIATION'S SECRET TO HIGH PERFORMANCE — 24

4. FROM THE AIR TO THE GROUND — 30
   Using Debrief to Lead and Win

## PART 3  WINNING WITH THE DAILY DEBRIEF

5. IMPROVE PERFORMANCE, ONE AREA AT A TIME — 36

6. THE G.R.E.A.T. DEBRIEF MODEL — 38
   Five Steps to High Performance

7. STEP 1 - GRATITUDE — 43
   High Performance Starts with Mind-Set

8. STEP 2 - REVIEW MISSION — 48
   Passion Comes from Purpose

9. STEP 3 - EVALUATE TODAY — 56
   Learn from Today to Win Tomorrow

10. STEP 4 - ANTICIPATE TOMORROW — 63
    Prepare to Win

11. STEP 5 - TIME FOR LESSONS LEARNED — 71
    Take Time to Learn and Grow

## PART 4  MAXIMIZING YOUR DAILY DEBRIEF

12. THE 5-MINUTE DAILY DEBRIEF — 80
    How to Be in the Top 5% in 5 Minutes a Day

13. CUSTOMIZING THE DAILY DEBRIEF — 86
    The Power of Personalized Debrief

## PART 5  THE DAILY DEBRIEF CHALLENGE

14. THE DAILY DEBRIEF CHALLENGE — 90
    28 Days to the Habit of High Performance

15. THE DAILY DEBRIEF CHALLENGE WORKBOOK — 93

CONCLUSION — 95

## APPENDIX

THE G.R.E.A.T DEBRIEF MODEL — 99
BOOK BONUSES — 100
THE DAILY DEBRIEF CHALLENGE - WEEK 1 — 101
ABOUT THE AUTHOR — 118

# Daily Debrief Book Bonuses

## Don't Miss These FREE Bonuses!

### www.Daily-Debrief.com/Book-Bonus

- A Customizable Daily Debrief 28-Day Challenge Workbook (to take debrief from a concept to a *habit*)

- Your Own Daily Debrief Mission Statement Builder (that teaches you *exactly* how to build a mission statement that gets *results*)

- The Daily Debrief High-Performance Assessment (so you can gain clarity on your unique *major impact* areas)

### www.Daily-Debrief.com/Book-Bonus

*To Cara, MacKenna, and CJ – Thank you for inspiring me to be better tomorrow than I am today.*

*The best way to predict your future is to create it.*
　　　　　—ABRAHAM LINCOLN

# Author's Note

Are you enjoying the success and prosperity you want?

If not, all that means is there's something you're not doing yet. You're missing one small piece of your puzzle, and once you find it, your life will catapult to the next level of success. This book is that missing piece.

In the pages that follow, you'll discover a habit that has the power to change your life. I realize that's a bold claim, yet I make it proudly because it's proven to be true. The simple five-step Daily Debrief routine contained in this book will transform your life by giving you a proven strategy to quickly and easily improve any area of your life.

This debrief model is based on the same strategy American fighter pilots use to consistently produce high-performance results. For over 25 years, I had the honor of serving as a fighter-attack pilot in both the US Marine Corps and US Air Force. While these elite organizations have a unique approach to accomplishing their mission, they share a commitment to improving performance through a detailed and disciplined practice of debrief. As both a pilot and a commander, I have been honored to see the concept of debrief produce extraordinary combat success from the deserts of Iraq to the mountains of Afghanistan.

While the Daily Debrief is based on the success secret of military aviation, it's designed to work in *your* life. By practicing the habit of debrief with this easy, step-by-step model, you *will* improve your performance in any area of life you choose—and improving your performance is the key to your success and prosperity.

For over a decade now, I have been helping people from all walks of life improve their performance through debrief. I have seen time and time again the powerful impact this simple habit called the Daily Debrief can have on someone's life. Not only does it work, it works quickly. In fact, one Daily Debrief practitioner recently told me, "The best thing about the Daily Debrief is that you can learn it today and see the results tomorrow."

So don't spend another day struggling to succeed simply because you lack a strategy to improve. Join me on this journey and let's discover how you can use military aviation's secret to high performance to lead and win—one debrief at a time!

Northern Arabian Gulf—Jeff "Bones" Bonner in an AV-8B Harrier just prior to launching on his first combat mission in Iraq.

(Photo courtesy of the author)

# Introduction

"Good luck, sir. This time, it's for real."

Those words, spoken just as I was about to launch from an aircraft carrier and head into my first combat mission, changed *everything* about my life.

As I lowered the crystal-clear canopy on the powerful fighter the Marine Corps had entrusted to me, I closed my eyes and thought, What if I'm not ready?

Then I thought about all the things that could go wrong: What if I hit the wrong target? What if I let down the Marines I'm here to protect? What if I get shot down, captured and held as a prisoner of war? What if I never see my wife and family again?

All these questions were running through my head and they led me to the greatest question of all—*What if I'm not good enough?*

Then I closed my eyes and said a little prayer—the same type of prayer so many say right before going into combat for the first time.

When I opened my eyes, two realities hit me. First, this wasn't about me. It was about those Marines—the 18-year-olds with their combat rifles who found themselves in a foreign land facing the greatest challenge of their young lives. That's who I was there for. I was there to serve them and others like them.

Second, I had trained for this. I knew what to do because I'd flown missions just like this one hundreds of times. More importantly, I'd debriefed missions just like this hundreds of times.

I wasn't going to fail, because I knew why I was there, who I was there for, and exactly what to do.

My newfound confidence was inspired by the fact that, years earlier, I had bought into a simple practice that consistently improves performance and outcomes. Through my training and experience as a fighter pilot, I had bought into the positive power of *debrief.*

To be certain, debrief in military aviation is very different from debrief in life. But when I started to debrief the important areas of my own life, things began to change for the better. In fact, I learned that this simple habit could improve every key area of my life.

As I started to apply the incredible simplicity of the debrief process, I learned that it wasn't always easy.

Figuring how to apply it consistently with little effort, ironically, took a lot of effort.

After years of perfecting this strategy and experiencing the success it produced in my own life, I started sharing it with others close to me. The results they experienced were amazing as well, not because of what I did, but because of the simplicity and power of this habit called the Daily Debrief.

I realized that a simple, powerful, and properly designed debrief strategy can change *anyone's* life for the better. So that's my goal for you—to help you take this simple habit and easily apply it so you can experience massive success and prosperity.

When you do, I'm certain everything will change for you. You'll be empowered to improve your career, your business, your family, your faith, your health, and your relationships. This debrief model will give you the ability to improve any and every area of your life you choose, quickly and easily.

One final note before we begin. It is with great humility and respect that I share the Daily Debrief with you. While I developed the Daily Debrief formula, the concept of improving performance through debrief is certainly not mine. I was simply fortunate enough to serve alongside some of the most talented fighter pilots in the world and I saw firsthand what made them elite.

Now I want to share their secret to high performance with you so you can use the concept of debrief to achieve your own success and prosperity.

So, what do you say? Are you ready to take the journey and improve your life with the Daily Debrief? Let's get going!

# PART 1

## It's Time to Win

# Chapter 1

# From the Treadmill to Prosperity

Have you ever felt stuck, like you're not moving forward as fast as you want? Like you're spinning your wheels and stuck on life's treadmill?

I know I have. We all have at one time or another. It's not fun, and it's not how life's supposed to be.

I believe we're all created with incredible potential. We are all created to achieve tremendous prosperity and success.

If you're not enjoying the prosperity and success you want, something has to change. It's not going to happen by itself.

Perhaps you've "tried it all before." You've attended the training seminars, read tons of books, and studied the "Greats of the World," but something just isn't working.

I learned the hard way that what's needed is *action*. But action isn't always easy to come by. In fact, without the right tools, action can be the hardest, most frustrating thing in the world.

With the right tools, however, anything is possible. Take starting a car—it would be very difficult if you didn't have a key. But with a key, the right tool, you can easily start the car and drive wherever you want to go.

It's the same with your life. The purpose of this book is to give you the one tool that will be your key to living a high-performance life. If you've ever felt stuck—and especially if you feel stuck now—this tool, the Daily Debrief, will be the key that unlocks your success and prosperity.

And all it takes is your action.

The good news is I'll guide you the whole way. All you need to do is start!

# Chapter 2

# The Daily Debrief Assessment

Have you ever heard the saying, "You've got to know where you are to know where you're going"? There's some serious truth to that.

To help you quickly and easily assess where you are in the individual areas of your life I recommend taking the Daily Debrief Assessment. The assessment is built around a powerful tool called the High-Performance Life Wheel and it's based on the idea that when we're living our best life, or our high-performance life, we are balanced and excelling in all of life's areas.

There are two ways you can take the assessment. You can visit www.Daily-Debrief.com/Book-Bonus and download a free version or you can take the assessment on the next page. And remember, there are no wrong answers. This is about awareness so you can improve the areas that are most important to you.

# The Daily Debrief Assessment

On a scale of 1-10, with 1 being poor and 10 being excellent, how would you rate the following areas of your life?

Career & Business

_____

Health & Wellness

_____

Love & Romance

_____

Fun & Recreation

_____

Finances

_____

Friends & Family

_____

Faith & Spirituality

_____

Contribution & Volunteering

_____

Now, simply plot your scores on the High-Performance Life Wheel by placing a dot on the circle corresponding to your score.

## The High-Performance Life Wheel

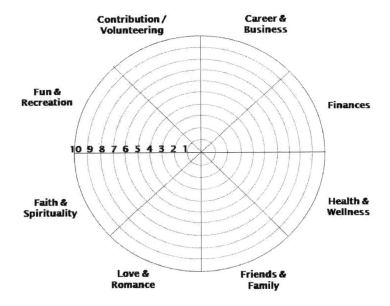

Now connect the dots. How does your wheel look? Is it balanced, with all the areas of your life at a level 10? If so, congratulations, you're living a high-performance life!

If, however, you're like most of us, your wheel isn't a perfect level 10 and you're not living your ideal life—at least not yet.

Actually, the first time most people do this exercise, their wheel looks a bit lopsided. They're doing well in some areas, and not so well in others. If that's you—and it certainly was me—don't worry. The first step to improvement is awareness. Now that you're aware, you're ready to dramatically improve your life.

That's what the Daily Debrief is designed to do. It will systematically improve your performance to take you from where you are now to living a high-performance life!

# PART 2

Discovering the Power of the Daily Debrief

# Chapter 3

# Debrief - Military Aviation's Secret to High Performance

A few years ago, I had the honor to attend Harvard University's Kennedy School of Government as a National Security Fellow. At the time, I had just returned from my second deployment to Afghanistan and was still very much in the military mind-set.

It was definitely a different feeling going from a fast-paced military environment to a fast-paced academic environment and to be honest, I struggled to make the transition. The pressure to perform academically was intense and I quickly found myself overwhelmed.

Remarkably, everything turned around for me after a conversation with a colleague in a cross-cultural leadership seminar. The seminar was about taking leadership principles that work in one area or discipline and applying them to another. It's an innovative concept that can really help leaders develop and produce extraordinary results.

So in the middle of this class, my colleague Jennifer leaned over and asked me: "How do you all do it?"

Jennifer knew I was a combat fighter pilot and former squadron commander. Basically, what she was asking was how fighter pilots are able to consistently perform at a high level in the fast-paced, dynamic environment of aerial combat.

Now, at that point in my career, I'd had the opportunity to work with different units from pretty much every branch of service in the military. Because of that, I knew the answer to her question right away.

I knew the answer lay in what fighter pilots do that nobody else does, at least certainly not to the level that we do.

So without much thought, I turned to Jennifer and said, "We improve our performance through debrief. That's how we do it. *Debriefing is military aviation's secret to high performance.*"

Now, I'm pretty sure she had heard about debriefing before and probably didn't think it was anything all that spectacular. In fact, she looked kind of puzzled as if to say, "Is that it?".

When I saw her skepticism, I told her that fighter pilots use the same performance model as everyone else, with one very important addition. I told her that most people, businesses, and organizations use some form of the Plan/Brief/Execute performance model.

Like most pilots, I am a visual person, so I took out a piece of paper and drew her a diagram. I said, "This is what most organizations do":

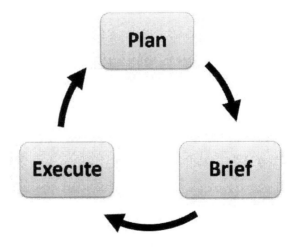

First, they develop a plan. They identify their goal and what they're trying to accomplish. They understand what and who is needed to complete their "mission." They create a timeline and objectives, and then assign roles.

Once they have a plan, they brief the team. They make sure everyone knows what they need to do, how to do it, what's expected of them, and when it needs to be done.

Then they execute. They go do what they've planned and briefed.

And that's where most people, businesses, and organizations stop. After they execute, they're done and they move on to the next crisis, project or task.

## Military Aviation's Secret to High Performance

In military aviation, we add one more critical step. That additional step makes fighter pilots safer, faster, and more effective than virtually any other group.

We debrief! So, in military aviation, our performance model looks like this:

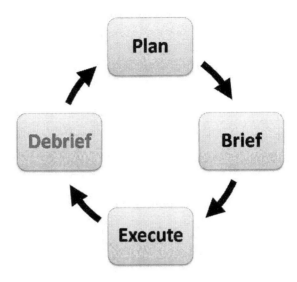

That's it. After *every* mission, we debrief—every time, without fail. And we are good at it, very good. In fact, we place such a focus on debriefing that it's not uncommon for our debriefs to take as long as the flight itself.

By adding the debrief step, we consistently improve our performance. Because we take the time to debrief, our next plan is better, our next brief is better, and our next execution is better.

Each flight and each mission improves the next one, and the cycle never ends. We consistently grow because we take the time to debrief our performance.

Now this time, I could see Jennifer got it. She understood the importance of debrief. But that only led her to say, "That's great that you guys debrief to improve your performance in the air, but *how do I use debrief to improve my performance on the ground?*"

And that question got me thinking...

# Chapter 4

# From the Air to the Ground

## Using Debrief to Lead and Win

As I thought about Jennifer's question and how she could use debrief to improve her performance, I thought perhaps I should do some experimentation in my own life.

So I asked myself what area of my life I would like to improve. That answer was simple.

As I mentioned earlier, at the time I was struggling academically and there was one course that was particularly challenging. The class was called The Art of Communication and it required students to give speeches on a variety of different subjects. During this class, it didn't take me long to realize that I was a terrible public speaker!

So, right then and there, I decided I was going to apply the debrief concept and see if I could improve my performance in public speaking.

My plan was to debrief my speech immediately after giving it to the class. The first time I did this, however, I quickly realized that I couldn't focus on my debrief because the next student was already speaking. Not to be rude or anything, but he was distracting my debrief!

What I needed was a quiet, private place where I could focus on capturing the lessons from the speech I had just given. Then it occurred to me . . . where is a quiet, private place that's in virtually every public building? Yes—the restroom!

So there I was, in a bathroom stall at the Harvard Kennedy School, debriefing the speech I had just given. It wasn't pretty, but it worked.

My debrief back then was pretty simple, just two questions:

1. What worked and how do I repeat it for the next speech?
2. What didn't work and how do I improve it for the next speech?

That was it. In just a few minutes, I captured the key lessons I needed to help me improve my performance for future speeches.

Now, I'm sure a few of my fellow classmates thought I had some sort of biological problem because I would disappear to the bathroom after every speech. But if they're reading this, now they know the truth!

All silliness aside, the thing is, it worked.

It was a real breakthrough to see that debriefing could be applied to improve my performance on the ground. Every speech I gave was a little bit better than the previous one just because I focused on what worked and what didn't.

## The Daily Debrief is Born

I didn't realize it at that time, but during that course, the Daily Debrief was born. Now that I had some success using debrief to improve my performance academically, I started to debrief other areas of my life.

I found that the technique worked every time I used it. At one point, I wanted to improve my health, so I debriefed my diet and exercise program—sure enough, my health improved.

Then I got curious about whether debriefing could help me be a better husband so, without telling my wife, I took time each night for a week and debriefed what I was doing to be the best husband I could be. Once again, it worked and my relationship with my wife improved.

Every single time I debriefed my performance, things improved. It didn't matter what area of my life I was focusing on: my health, my relationships, my finances, my career—it all got better. Simply by adopting the habit of debriefing, I began improving my life in remarkable ways.

At this point, I knew debriefing could be used by anyone to improve their performance in any area of life. So over the next few years, I continued debriefing my own life and developed a model that produced the maximum results in the minimum time. That model is called the Daily Debrief, and I assure you it will work for you just like it has for so many others.

So now let's dive into exactly what this Daily Debrief habit is and how you can use it to improve *your* life!

# PART 3

## Winning with the Daily Debrief

## Chapter 5

# Improve Performance, One Area at a Time

The Daily Debrief is a habit that's practiced each evening before you go to bed. It's designed to use the power of focus to improve a single area of your life each week.

Why one area a week?

The science of human performance tells us that if we focus on one thing consistently over a period of seven days, it allows us enough time to make progress and improve. Any longer than a week, and we risk letting the other areas of our life fall behind. A week is the perfect amount of time to focus on improving a single life area.

How do you know which life area you want to focus on this week?

Let's go back to your High-Performance Life Wheel that you completed as part of your Daily Debrief Assessment in Chapter Two. When you look at your wheel, which area stands out as the one you want to improve? It doesn't have to be the area that needs the most work; it could simply be the area that's most important to you right now.

So what's one specific area of your life you would like to improve this week? Is it your finances? Your health? Your career?

Choose the area you want to improve this week and write it down now.

**This week I will focus on improving my**

_____.


Great! So now that you've identified your area of improvement, it's time to introduce you to the five-step Daily Debrief model that will unlock your high-performance life!

## Chapter 6

# The G.R.E.A.T. Debrief Model

### Five Steps to High Performance

The Daily Debrief is built around a simple five-step evening routine called the G.R.E.A.T. Debrief Model.

I'm one of those people who absolutely love acronyms. I guess it's because I spent my career in the military, where we have an acronym for just about everything. In the Marine Corps, I learned that a good acronym has the power to simplify concepts by making them easy to remember.

So when you think of the five-step Daily Debrief, keep in mind the acronym G.R.E.A.T.

Step 1 - **G**ratitude

Step 2 - **R**eview Mission

Step 3 - **E**valuate Today

Step 4 - **A**nticipate Tomorrow

Step 5 - **T**ime For Lessons Learned

These five steps will keep you on track with the Daily Debrief and accelerate your progress toward improving your performance.

So here's a quick overview of how the Daily Debrief works:

Each evening before you go to bed, you'll go through the five-step model and debrief the day you just lived. In Step 1, you'll prepare yourself for high performance by establishing an attitude of gratitude. In Step 2, you'll unleash your passion by clarifying your purpose. In Step 3, you'll ask yourself key questions to evaluate your day. In Step 4, you'll prepare yourself for tomorrow's success by identifying easily achievable goals and anticipating their accomplishment. Finally, in Step 5, you'll take time out to ensure you capture the key lessons necessary for your future success.

That's it. Those five simple steps of the Daily Debrief will improve your performance and accelerate your path to success.

Are you ready? Let's get into each step in more detail and get you on your way to living your high-performance life!

*High performance starts with an attitude of gratitude.*

## CHAPTER 7

# Step 1 – Gratitude

## HIGH PERFORMANCE STARTS WITH MIND-SET

One thing I learned flying in combat is that to achieve high performance you must first be in the right state of mind. So I want to share with you what I have found is the key to a winning mind-set:

***High performance starts with an attitude of gratitude.***

Make no mistake—your road to winning starts with being grateful for where you are right now.

I first learned about the power gratitude has to improve performance in the moments before my first aircraft carrier landing.

For Navy and Marine Corps pilots, landing on the aircraft carrier, or "The Boat," as we call it, is the final stage of a two-year fighter pilot training program. It's special because, as the graduation event, the stakes are high and there is tremendous pressure to perform.

The first time I went to The Boat, I went with two other students, each of us alone in our own aircraft. We took off from a naval air station in Florida and were led to the USS John F. Kennedy by our flight lead, Lieutenant Commander Greg "Pee-wee" Herman.

The flight out to the aircraft carrier was quiet—all three of us were nervous about what was about to happen. But things quickly changed when we arrived overhead the carrier. I will never forget as I looked down and saw that tiny aircraft carrier floating atop the expanse of the Atlantic Ocean.

At that point, I was certain the Marine Corps had made a colossal mistake and I was in the wrong place. There was no way I was going to be able to land on that little ship.

Then, the voice of our flight lead interrupted my mental meltdown. Through his experience, Pee-wee knew we were all having the same doubts and that none of us were in the right state of mind for peak performance. So, to change our focus, he said, "Fellas, how fortunate are we to be here right now? Do you know how many people in the world would love to be where you are?"

In an instant, my mind-set changed. I'd been so focused on my problems, I hadn't considered that there were people who would actually love to face the challenge I was facing. I was, in fact, very fortunate to be there.

Then he continued, "Your government has sailed this ship out here just for you to land on. This is what you've trained for—right here, right now. Let's go do it."

And that's what we did. Like all naval aviators, I will never forget the experience of landing on the aircraft carrier for the first time.

But the other thing I'll never forget about my first carrier landing is how gratitude put me in the right mind-set for peak performance.

## Let Gratitude Be Your Fuel

I know you want to improve your performance and enjoy more success. I know you want to lead and win in life. If you didn't, you wouldn't still be here on this journey with me.

But the reality is, to improve your life you must start by being thankful for where you are right now. *The road to making things better begins with realizing things could always be worse.*

When I speak to audiences about the Daily Debrief, I show them a picture I took returning from a mission in northern Afghanistan. It's an aerial photo of the capital city of Kabul I took from the cockpit of my A-10 Thunderbolt. I use that photo as a powerful reminder of how fortunate I am. The people of Kabul, Afghanistan are challenged by living in a country of war and poverty. I am blessed to live in a country of peace and prosperity.

I use that photo to constantly remind myself that no matter how bad things are, my worst day is better than many people's best day. I have so much to be grateful for—no matter how bad it is, it could always be worse.

So, let me ask you:

***What are you grateful for right now?***

It doesn't have to be something huge. In fact, it's better if it's something small or simple. It's all about establishing the winning mind-set. When you put yourself in the right mind-set, you unleash the power of high performance.

So right now, it's time for some action. (Remember, *nothing* happens without action.)Before you do anything else, list three things you're grateful for.

**Three things I'm grateful for right now are**

- _____
- _____
- _____

Remember, gratitude and high performance go hand in hand. Gratitude is the first step to putting yourself in the high-performance mind-set, so please don't skip this step!

OK, so now that you're in a winning state of mind, let's go to Step 2 and unleash your passion by clarifying your purpose.

## Chapter 8

# Step 2 – Review Mission

### Passion Comes From Purpose

What's your "why"?

I'm betting you've heard that question a thousand times by now.

Well it may be the most important question you'll ever be asked. That's because it's the question that will unleash your passion and inspire you to take action.

Why do you do what you do? Why do you wake up in the morning? Why do you want prosperity and success?

If you're like most people, you probably don't have a clear answer. Don't worry. That's what this step of the Daily Debrief is all about!

When trying to determine your why, the most powerful tool I know of is a clearly worded mission statement.

I saw the positive power of a mission statement as a fighter-attack pilot in Iraq and Afghanistan. Every combat mission I flew started with one.

For example, when I was flying out of Bagram Air Base in northern Afghanistan, we were frequently tasked to support Special Operations Forces as they conducted raids on "high-value targets."

Most of these raids took place in the middle of the night so we could take advantage of our superior night vision capabilities, both in the air and on the ground. These were dangerous, high-risk raids. The Special Operations Forces on the ground needed to rely on air support without fail.

To make sure we had everything we needed for success, we would develop a mission statement for each operation. So, for example, if we were tasked to support US Navy SEALs conducting a midnight raid, our mission statement might be: "Tonight's mission is to provide close air support to US Special Operations Forces in order to capture Objective X (Code Name of High-Value Target)."

With that simple, clear mission statement we had our why. We knew why we were taking off and exactly what we needed to accomplish.

And every single time, our mission statement would guide us. Each mission statement gave us a clear understanding of how we needed to load the aircraft. It told us exactly what weapons and tactics we'd need to accomplish the mission. It guided the strategy we used to give us the best chance of success, and so on.

But most importantly, whenever we faced a problem, we'd go back to our mission statement and adapt the plan to accomplish the mission. It always came back to the mission statement. It was our "shining star" to follow. It was our guide.

And guess what? It worked. Our clearly defined mission statement was a critical key to our battlefield success.

## Defining Your Mission

Unfortunately, very few of us have mission statements to guide our life. We go from crisis to crisis, "putting out fires," because we don't have a clearly defined guideline of what success looks like. We plow through the day, moving from task to task, hammering away at our to-do list. And while it's usually important stuff, it's often not necessarily aligned with our purpose and what we want for our life.

That's not what I want for you. I want you to be in complete control of your day and your life. The best way I know to do that is to develop a clearly defined mission statement.

## How to Develop Your Mission Statement

To get you started on your mission statement, here is a simple but effective template.

*My mission is to_____in order to _____.*

This is a great template because it captures the two most important parts of any mission statement: what and why.

Let's look at each part more closely.

## Discovering Your What

The first part of a mission statement is your "what"—that is, what you want to do. This part of your mission statement should clearly describe the actions you want to take to make your life meaningful. Here, you want to use powerful action words. Words like *inspire*, *create*, and *empower* are often used by Daily Debrief practitioners in their mission statements.

If this is your first time trying to narrow down what you want to do, I know it can be overwhelming. To help, you can go to www.Daily-Debrief.com/Book-Bonus and download the free Daily Debrief Mission Statement Builder. That guide has a helpful list of commonly used action words you can use for inspiration when developing your mission statement.

## Defining Your Why

The second part of your mission statement is your "why"—that is, why you are taking action. When defining your why, think about your ideal vision for the future. What's your purpose for taking action? What kind of world are you trying to create for yourself and others? That's your why.

Here's the same advice I give to people who are developing their mission statements for the first time: Make sure you have a purpose that's greater than yourself. You have unique skills, passions, and abilities. Use them, not only to improve your own life, but to improve the lives of others around you. Commit to a mission that's greater than your own self-interest and *you will* live a life of happiness, passion, and purpose.

## Putting Your Mission Statement Together

To complete your mission statement, simply put your what and why together using the template. For example, when I developed my mission statement, my what was to "serve, lead, and inspire others." My why was to "create a safe and prosperous world for all." So when I put those two together, my mission statement became: My mission is to serve, lead, and inspire others to create a safe and prosperous world for all.

There are two important things to keep in mind when you're developing a mission statement. First, it's a process. Your initial mission statement will not be your last. It can, and should, change as you think about what you want to do in your life and why you want to do it.

Second, keep in mind that you can and should have more than one mission statement. So far, we've covered developing a life mission statement, but you can use the same template for any kind of mission statement. For example, as you use the Daily Debrief to improve a specific area of your life, your mission statement template will be:

*My mission is to improve my_____ in order to _____.*

Here you start with your weekly area of focus. What part of your life will you improve this week with the Daily Debrief? That goes in the first blank.

The second blank is for your why. Why do you want to improve that area of your life?

Let's say you want to improve your health. In that case, your Daily Debrief mission statement may be: My mission is to improve my health in order to have the energy and vitality to play with my kids.

Or, if you want to improve your finances, your mission statement may be: My mission is to improve my finances in order to become financially free so I can work because I want to, not because I have to.

## A Quick Step to Move You in the Right Direction

Before you go on to the next chapter, write a first draft of your mission statement for clarity and purpose. Again, you can visit www.Daily-Debrief.com/Book-Bonus and download a free mission statement builder for ideas and inspiration.

***My mission is to*** _____

_____ ***in order to***

_____.

Don't worry if it's not perfect yet—you're going for progress, not perfection.

Now that you have a clearly defined mission statement, let's go to Step 3, where you'll learn a battle-proven technique to evaluate your performance in a way that's guaranteed to produce future success.

## CHAPTER 9

# Step 3 – Evaluate Today

### LEARN FROM TODAY TO WIN TOMORROW

After you've established the winning mind-set of gratitude in Step 1 and clarified your mission in Step 2, it's time to evaluate your day.

In military aviation, an important part of our success is our ability to determine what happened so we can apply what we've learned. That's how fighter pilots consistently get better and improve their performance.

## How Military Aviators Captures Lessons Learned

As fighter pilots, when we debrief, we ask *questions*. We ask the right questions to get the right answers—the answers that are necessary to make us better.

The first question we always ask is, "Did we accomplish our mission?" It sounds simple, but it's important. We have to know whether we did what we set out to do. This question always has a simple yes or no answer. Either we got the job done or we didn't, and we need to be clear about it.

The second question we ask is, "What worked, and how do we repeat it?" If something worked, it's important to identify it so we can make sure we do it again next time. Success leaves clues and it's our job to find them.

The third and final question we ask is, "What didn't work, and how do we improve it"? We need to know specifically what isn't working so we can fix it for next time. This question often leads to our biggest breakthroughs in performance because it's through our failures that we grow.

So, the idea is, if we can be clear about our mission accomplishment, do more of what works, and improve what doesn't, we *will* be better next time. It's pretty simple, right?

Because of the proven success of this technique in military aviation, the Daily Debrief uses the same three simple questions to evaluate our day:

1. Did I accomplish my mission?
2. What worked, and how do I repeat it?
3. What didn't work, and how do I improve it?

I can tell you with certainty that this method of debriefing works. It's proven to improve performance for fighter pilots and it will improve performance for you.

Now let's take a closer look at each question.

### *Did I accomplish my mission?*

Did you know that when fighter pilots ask themselves this question in training, the answer is frequently no?

Here's the reason: We push ourselves to fail in training so we don't fail in combat—but we always learn from our failures. In other words, we push ourselves to the limit so we can develop and improve. Pushing to the point of failure forces us to expand and grow, and that's why, in my totally biased opinion, American fighter pilots are the best in the world.

I share this with you because of something I learned observing others as they practiced the Daily Debrief. When evaluating your performance, it's easy to get down on yourself, but you shouldn't. Most of the time, it means you're stretching yourself, which is a very good thing. That's called growth, and growth can be messy. So don't get discouraged. If you don't accomplish your mission on any given day, simply debrief it, learn from it, and move on.

### *What worked, and how do I repeat it?*

When you ask yourself this question, you're looking for three things that went well. Think about where you "won" today. What were the moments you're most proud of?

The important point is to find *three* things you did well. By identifying three successes from today, you can work to repeat them tomorrow.

### *What didn't work, and how do I improve it?*

When it comes time to look at what didn't work so well, find *one* thing. It can be small, or it can be big. Find one thing that happened today that didn't go as well as you would like and ask yourself how you can do it better tomorrow.

This third question could be the most important part of the entire Daily Debrief. Why? Because success begins with failure.

Think of something you're very good at—even great at. Were you always great at it? I bet you weren't. You became great by making mistakes, learning from them, and getting better.

It's the same with every area of your life and business. If you want to achieve greater success and prosperity, you have to look at the parts that didn't go well. Often, it's in those moments that the keys to success are hidden.

## Why Find Three Things That Worked and Only One That Didn't?

There's a reason for everything. And in the case of the Daily Debrief, there's a reason we find three things that worked and only one that didn't.

It comes straight from the US Marine Corps' three-to-one principle of overwhelming force. Overwhelming force is a battle-tested and proven concept that's used by the Marine Corps to win.

The Marines do not believe in a "fair fight." The only fight Marines are interested in is the kind where they win and the enemy loses. Period.

To ensure that happens, Marines use overwhelming force. How much force is necessary to be overwhelming? Ideally, Marines strive for a force three times the size of their enemies. So, for example, if they're going up against a force of one hundred enemy combatants, they'll want to use three hundred Marines to achieve victory.

In fact, the Marine Corps is organized and built around this three-to-one principle. The basic element of the Marine Corps is a fire team. Three fire teams make one squad, three squads make a platoon, three platoons make a company, and so on.

This organization and the three-to-one principle make it easy for the Marine Corps to provide overwhelming force and win. If they're facing a squad-sized enemy force, they use a platoon. If they're facing a platoon-sized enemy force, they'll use a company.

What's the point, other than some good Marine Corps organizational knowledge?

You've got to use overwhelming force to win. You can't get caught up in the negative parts of your day. Overwhelm every one negative with three positives and, like the Marine Corps, you'll consistently improve your performance and win.

OK, so now it's time for some action. It's time to evaluate your day in a way that will make you better tomorrow. When you think about your day, ask yourself:

1. *Did I live my mission today?*

2. *What worked, and how do I repeat it?*

- _____
- _____
- _____

3. *What didn't work, and how do I improve it?*

- _____

Now that you've evaluated your day in a way that will improve your performance, you're ready for Step 4. You're ready for the all-important step of preparing yourself to win!

## Chapter 10

# Step 4 – Anticipate Tomorrow

### PREPARE TO WIN

One thing I learned while flying fighters in combat is that winning doesn't happen by luck or happenstance. Winning requires a commitment to consistently improve performance. It also requires a specific process that prepares you for success. That's what Step 4 of the Daily Debrief is all about—giving you a process that will prepare you to win.

First, a quick review.

So far, you've created a high-performance mind-set by identifying three things you're grateful for (Step 1). You've reviewed your mission statement (Step 2) and evaluated your day by finding what worked and what you want to improve (Step 3).

Now, the most powerful step.

It's impossible to overstate the positive power of anticipating your future. Nothing will have a bigger impact on your success than a clear vision of your future.

To make it simple, this step of the Daily Debrief is broken down into two easy parts.

## Part 1: Identify Your Daily 3

First, identify your Daily 3. What are these, you ask?

Well, your Daily 3 are three *simple*, *specific*, and *easily achievable* tasks you can do tomorrow that will improve performance in your chosen area.

Let's take a closer look at each element of the Daily 3.

### Keep It Simple
Complexity kills progress. The easier something is to do, the more likely you are to do it. Your Daily 3 should be very simple tasks.

**Be Specific**
Ambiguity leads to inaction; specificity leads to achievement. Make your three tasks specific. (Hint: if you're having trouble making them specific, it's probably because they aren't simple enough.)

**Make it Easily Achievable**
You're setting yourself up to win tomorrow, not struggle through your day. The tasks you set should be easily achievable. Don't underestimate the power that achieving small goals has on your ability to achieve big goals.

The idea behind the Daily 3 is that you're looking for small wins—lots and lots of small wins. At the end of each day, I want you to have three victories (remember the concept of overwhelming force in the last chapter?).

Trust me on this: the practice of completing three simple, specific, and easily achievable tasks each day will create a tidal wave of momentum that will quickly push you to success.

## Part 2: Chair Fly Your Success

After you've laid out your Daily 3, it's time to go through a process of visualization where you actually *see* yourself succeeding.

If you're new to visualization, bear with me here because it works. Ask any great athlete or performer and they'll tell you they always see the achievement in their mind before they accomplish it.

I learned about the power visualization has on success as a young fighter-attack pilot in the Marine Corps. Believe me, when you're flying at 500 miles per hour, 300 feet above the ground, things happen fast. The only way to slow things down is what fighter pilots call "chair flying."

Chair flying in military aviation is a simple but effective method of visualization. Basically, before each mission, we mentally rehearse the flight we're about to do. We visualize every part of it. Every portion of the mission from engine start to engine shutdown is rehearsed in our minds.

We go over airspeeds, altitudes, formations, weapons we'll be using, and so on. All of these tasks are rehearsed *first* in our minds while sitting in a chair at zero miles per hour. Why? So when we do it for real, we've seen it all before. We've pictured it in our minds and know exactly what we're doing.

When I was in Iraq and Afghanistan, the single greatest contributor to success was the quality of my pre-mission visualization. Without question, it was a powerful key to achieving high performance and overall mission success.

## Chair Flying Works the Same in Life

What I learned in creating the Daily Debrief was that this exact same process works just as well in daily life. When we take time to visualize our success for tomorrow, we are far more likely to achieve it.

It will work the same for you. So each night, after you've identified tomorrow's Daily 3, visualize yourself completing them.

Now, this process may feel a bit strange the first few times you do it, but trust me—it will be the most powerful thing you do to transform your life and achieve the success you want.

## How to Chair Fly Your Success

To chair fly your success start with the first of your Daily 3 tasks. Close your eyes and see yourself getting ready to accomplish it. Picture it like you're watching a video of yourself completing the task. See yourself in the moment, making it happen. Most importantly, see yourself succeeding.

Now, do the same thing for the other two tasks.

If you don't take time to see yourself succeeding, it's easy to get caught up in the chaos of the day. That's like flying 500 miles per hour without rehearsing what you'll see. Things will happen way too fast and you'll be reactive throughout the day. That's a recipe for disaster!

## An Optional Step: Review Your Vision Board

One additional step I recommend to particularly ambitious Daily Debrief practitioners is to develop a vision board.

If you're brand new to vision boards, just know that they're simply a collage of all the things you want to accomplish. These aren't necessarily only material things, but nonmaterial things as well.

Vision boards, or dream boards as they're sometimes called, are a powerful way to focus your mind on what you want—and we all know that what we focus on expands!

**Creating Your Vision Board**

To create your vision board, go online and find some pictures that represent each area of your high-performance life. Then, cut and paste them on a single PowerPoint slide and, just like that, you've got your vision board.

These should be all the things you want in your life—houses, cars, career experiences, places to visit, people to meet, goals to accomplish, and so on. Put whatever you want on there. Have fun putting it together and remember to think big!

Here's a final note on vision boards. When making your board, remember to find at least one image of what you want for each area of your high-performance life. That way, you'll have a clear vision of success in every aspect of your life.

Now it's time for action. Let's apply what you've learned about improving your performance by anticipating the future.

## Part 1: Identify Your Daily 3

What are three *simple, specific and easily achievable* tasks that you can do to be better tomorrow?

1. _____

2. _____

3. _____

## Part 2: Chair Fly Your Success

Visualize accomplishing tomorrow's Daily 3.

## Optional Step: Review Your Vision Board

Create a collage of images that represents success in each of your important life areas.

Excellent! You now have a proven process that will consistently prepare you to win. Next, it's time for the fifth and final step of the Daily Debrief. It's time to reflect on the bigger picture and capture the lessons you've learned.

## Chapter 11

# Step 5 – Time For Lessons Learned

TAKE TIME TO LEARN AND GROW

If you're into sports, you know time-outs are an important part of the game. It's during time-outs that teams slow things down, reflect on what's happening, and plan their next play to win.

So guess what's next for you?

The final step in the Daily Debrief is to call your own time-out, slow things down, and set yourself up to win.

Here's why it works.

Most days we're moving from one crisis to another. We wake up, check our phones, rush through breakfast, get out of the house, get stuck in traffic, and hurry into work. Once we get to work, we're rushing from meeting to meeting or task to task. When the day ends, we rush home, have a quick dinner, maybe watch some TV, spend a little time with family, and then head to bed.

And it's off to the next day—wash, rinse, and repeat.

What we really need, as counterintuitive as it may sound, is a time-out. We need to slow things down, capture the lessons we've learned, and reflect on what's important.

Life's busy, and at first glance, it's hard to take time to reflect. But we all make time for what's important. And taking a time-out at the end of your Daily Debrief will pay for itself—over and over.

## How to Take a Time Out

Over the years, I've found the very best way to take a time-out and reflect is through journaling. What's great about journaling is that when you capture the moments of the day you just lived, you gain a powerful perspective on your life. It's insightful to see the changes as you go from day to day, and it adds a huge amount of awareness.

The only rule with journaling is there are no rules! Just write. Write about what you feel compelled to write about. There's nothing too big and nothing too small. The only goal is to capture your thoughts about your day. It's a great way to track your successes and struggles, and over time, you'll see that you've had way more successes than struggles.

Have you ever heard that you can't measure progress without knowing where you started? That's especially true when you're out to live a high-performance life. You have to know where you started and where you've been along the journey. Trust me on this: you'll be thrilled to have this record down the road. It's one of the single greatest opportunities sitting in front of you today.

## Capturing Your Lessons Learned

One of the best things you'll find in your journal is how you overcame obstacles along your path to success. These observations are called your "Lessons Learned" and they're a major part of your success.

The wisdom you gain from your lessons learned is part of your legacy. By capturing it in your Daily Debrief, you're recording your secrets to success for future generations—and it doesn't get any bigger than that!

There are lots of ways to journal, but the easiest and most convenient way to do it as part of your Daily Debrief is with the Daily Debrief Journal. It's specifically designed to walk you through all five steps of the Daily Debrief and it's a great place to record your lessons learned. You can find the Daily Debrief Journal at www.Daily-Debrief.com.

Another option is a digital journal. If you prefer the ease and convenience of using a digital journal, you can choose from literally dozens of apps that are excellent for capturing your life's journey. Of course, the great thing about these digital journals is that they're always with you, right there on your phone.

Whichever journal you use, know that your high-performance life starts today! It's the beginning of your new road to success. Later, you'll enjoy looking back and seeing where it all started.

## Capture Your Lessons Learned

So guess what time it is? You guessed it—it's time for action. Right now, make your first journal entry. It doesn't have to be long; just write about what's going on in your life to keep your positive momentum before moving on.

## Step 5 – Time For Lessons Learned

What were today's lessons learned?

**Congratulations! Your Daily Debrief is complete!**

Now that you've learned all five steps of the Daily Debrief, in the next few chapters you'll discover how to maximize the process to achieve your highest levels of success and prosperity.

# PART 4

## Maximizing Your Daily Debrief

## Chapter 12

# The 5-Minute Daily Debrief

### How to Be in the Top 5% in 5 Minutes a Day

When I started sharing the Daily Debrief with others, the first thing I noticed was that it worked.

The second thing I noticed was that it can be challenging to commit thirty minutes a day to a new habit.

If that sounds like something you can relate to, here's the 5-Minute Daily Debrief.

Can five minutes a day really make a difference? Absolutely! And not just that, but it'll help you see the power of debrief and motivate you to keep going. (Remember the small, simple wins?)

## What's Your Excuse?

The number one reason people don't debrief is *time*. I get it. I do. Time is the most precious commodity we have and when we're running from crisis to crisis, it feels like we never have enough.

In fact, lack of time is why most people and organizations don't debrief—ever. But do you know what the top 5 percent always do? You guessed it: they debrief their performance *daily*.

So do you want to be common, or do you want to join the top 5 percent? Since you're still reading, we both know the answer to that!

## The 5-Minute Daily Debrief

So now you're going to learn how to apply the five-minute version of the Daily Debrief. Here's how it works.

You'll go through the same five-step G.R.E.A.T. Debrief Model we covered in Part Three. The only difference is that each step will be abbreviated so you'll get the maximum benefit in the minimum amount of time. You're going to spend one minute on each step.

Here's the five-minute breakdown:

**Minute 1: Gratitude**

Get yourself in the high-performance mind-set by finding one thing, big or small, that you're grateful for right now. What's one thing you feel fortunate to have in your life? Think about how thankful you are for it and what your life would be like without it.

One thing I'm grateful for right now is

_____

**Minute 2: Review Your Mission**

My mission is to _____

_____.

## Minute 3: Evaluate Today's Performance

When you think about your day, ask yourself three questions:

1. Did I accomplish my mission?   Yes / No

2. What worked?

    Three things that went well today were

- _____
- _____
- _____

3. What didn't work?

    One thing that didn't go well today was

- _____

Your goal is to find three good things to repeat and one thing to improve. In my decades of debriefing, I can tell you that simply identifying your successes and struggles is 80 percent of improving performance.

## Minute 4: Anticipate Tomorrow's Success

1. Identify your Daily 3

What are three simple, specific, and easily achievable tasks you can do tomorrow to improve your performance?

- _____
- _____
- _____

2. Chair fly success

    Visualize accomplishing each of your Daily 3.

## Minute 5: Time For Lessons Learned

To wrap things up, take a minute to capture your lessons learned in a journal. It doesn't have to be a lot, and don't worry about grammar or spelling. Simply write about whatever you learned today and how you will be better tomorrow.

## That's it!

In just five minutes, you've completed all five steps of the Daily Debrief. You started by creating an attitude of gratitude. Next, you reviewed your mission for clarity and purpose. Then, you evaluated your day to capture the good and the bad. You anticipated a successful tomorrow by identifying your Daily 3. Finally, you took time out to record the journey.

Well done! Your Daily Debrief is complete and you just spent the most productive five minutes of your day.

# Chapter 13

# Customizing the Daily Debrief

## The Power of Personalized Debrief

As a fighter-attack pilot, I've found that the difference between a good performance model and a great one is that great performance models can be adapted to fit each unique situation.

That's why the Daily Debrief is specifically designed to be customized to fit *your* life. In this chapter, we'll cover two of the most common ways you can personalize the Daily Debrief for maximum success.

## 1. Customizing Your High-Performance Life Wheel

The first way to customize the Daily Debrief is with a personalized High-Performance Life Wheel. Because your ideal life is different from everyone else's, your Life Wheel should be different as well.

If you visit www.Daily-Debrief.com/Book-Bonus you can download both the preformatted wheel like the one used here in the book and a customizable High-Performance Life Wheel.

The good news about the preformatted wheel is that it covers the areas that are important to most of our lives (Family, Career, Finances, Health, and so on).

With the customized wheel, however, you have the freedom to define the areas that are most important to you. For example, if your high-performance life includes being a spouse, parent, and business owner, you can fill in the wheel to include a category for each of these areas. This allows you to ensure your wheel reflects all the important areas of *your* life.

The key point when customizing your wheel is that whatever areas make up your ideal life should have their own category.

2. **Customizing Your Time**

Another great way you can customize the Daily Debrief is with the time and attention you devote to each of the debrief steps.

If after completing a week of the Daily Debrief you realize you get the most benefit from cultivating an attitude of gratitude, you'll want to spend more time in Step 1 (Gratitude).

Or maybe you get the most out of capturing your lessons learned through journaling. If so, Step 5 (Time For Lessons Learned) is where you'll want to spend more of your time.

Personally, I get the most out of visualizing my future success in Step 4 (Anticipate Tomorrow), so that's where I spend the most time.

No matter how you use it, the Daily Debrief should be unique to *you*. It's a tool—a very effective one—to improve your performance so you can lead and win. But to be most effective, it has to be customized for *you*. So go ahead and make it yours!

# PART 5

The Daily Debrief Challenge

## Chapter 14

# The Daily Debrief Challenge

### 28 Days to the Habit of High Performance

Now that you know how the Daily Debrief works (and how you can do it in just five minutes a day), it's time to put it to good use.

But first, let me ask you something.

If you could *really* change the entire trajectory of your life in 28 days, would you commit to the handful of minutes a day it takes to develop a new habit?

Now, you've made it this far, so I know the answer is yes! The challenge is that, to improve your life, you have to go beyond simply learning new techniques or concepts.

You have to put them into action!

No matter how great your new knowledge is, your life will only improve through *action*. That's it. Everything else is just window dressing.

If you don't take action to make your life better, you'll keep getting the same things you have right now—and I know you want more. So to help you install this new habit, here's the 28-Day Daily Debrief Challenge.

## 28 Days to the Habit of High Performance

Will you commit to doing the Daily Debrief for the next 28 days?

Over the next four weeks, focus on improving four areas of your life. Improve just one area each week.

This means you'll choose a total of four areas of your High-Performance Life Wheel to improve. Don't worry if there's more you want to accomplish—this is just the start of your Daily Debrief habit.

Now, just like anything new, it's going to get easier and easier the more you do it. Be patient with yourself and start with the 5-Minute Daily Debrief. (Small wins, remember?).

Things really will begin to happen when you get into week two. By then you'll be accustomed to the routine, you'll be more comfortable with the process, and you'll already be seeing some improvements.

By the time week three rolls around, you'll be hooked. Why? Because you'll have tangible results in your life that show the power of the Daily Debrief.

What will happen when you get to week four? Well, you'll be shocked by the change in your life in such a short period of time. You'll have seen firsthand the power the Daily Debrief has to improve your performance and you'll be fired up to keep it a part of your nightly routine.

And because you've been journaling each night in Step 5 (Time For Lessons Learned), at the end of 28 days, you'll have some amazing discoveries to look back on. You'll have a record of the progress you made and it'll be something you can continue going back to for inspiration.

Your life will improve, not when you learn something new, but when you *do* something new. Let today be that day, the day you start a new habit that will lead you down a new road—the road to your success and prosperity!

## Chapter 15

# The Daily Debrief Challenge Workbook

Completing the 28-Day Daily Debrief Challenge is, by far, the most important part of this book. Why? Because completing the challenge transforms the Daily Debrief from a theoretical concept to an actionable *habit*.

Remember, your life will not improve simply because you learn something new. Your life will improve because you *do* something new.

So, to help you take action and install the Daily Debrief as a new habit, this workbook will guide you, day by day, through all 28 days of the challenge. To get you started, the first week of the challenge workbook is included in the Appendix. You can download the full 28-day workbook for free at www.Daily-Debrief.com/Book-Bonus.

Each night, before you go to bed, take a few minutes and debrief your day. Use this workbook to walk yourself through each step of the G.R.E.A.T. Debrief Model so you can quickly and easily complete your Daily Debrief.

Please don't let the Daily Debrief be just another concept that you learn but never use. Take a few minutes a day for the next 28 days and give yourself the gift of a new success habit. You're just a month away from living your high-performance life!

## Conclusion

We all have moments of change in our lives—moments that define who we are and change who we will become.

For me, one of those moments was sitting on the deck of that aircraft carrier, getting ready to launch on my first combat mission. In that moment, I learned a life lesson that has shaped who I am. Right there, off the coast of Iraq, I realized that it's not about me. It's about those I'm here to serve.

It's in that spirit of service that I share with you the Daily Debrief. My greatest wish for you is that this habit changes your life in profound and measurable ways. Use it to unleash the high-performance life that will create all the success and prosperity you so richly deserve.

I want you to have all the treasures and achievements you dream of. I want you and your family to be happy, healthy, and wealthy. In short, I want you to lead and win in every area of your life.

And I know you can have these things. You weren't made to struggle or to just do well; you were made to achieve abundant success. But I also know that these things don't come easy. To get more, you have to become more; you have to consistently improve. And when you make progress each day—even if it's just a little bit—you end up way better than you ever thought possible.

That's why I am sharing the Daily Debrief: so that by adopting this simple habit, you can improve each day and achieve success beyond your wildest dreams!

It's a great honor to share military aviation's secret to high performance with you. I thank you for your commitment of time and focus. I hope someday we get a chance to meet in person and you can tell me about how you used the Daily Debrief to achieve your goals and live the life of your dreams.

Now it's time to put what you've learned into action. It's time to practice and share this simple, five-step habit called the Daily Debrief. When you do, you'll unleash the power of your own high performance—one debrief at a time!

To your success and prosperity,

# APPENDIX

# THE G.R.E.A.T DEBRIEF MODEL

Step 1 - **G**ratitude

Step 2 - **R**eview Mission

Step 3 - **E**valuate Today
       1. What worked?
       2. What didn't work?

Step 4 - **A**nticipate Tomorrow
       1. How can it be better next time?

Step 5 - **T**ime For Lessons Learned

## DAILY DEBRIEF BOOK BONUSES

# Don't Miss These FREE Bonuses!

### www.Daily-Debrief.com/Book-Bonus

- A Customizable Daily Debrief 28-Day Challenge Workbook (to take debrief from a concept to a *habit*)

- Your Own Daily Debrief Mission Statement Builder (that teaches you *exactly* how to build a mission statement that gets *results*)

- The Daily Debrief High-Performance Assessment (so you can gain clarity on your unique *major impact* areas)

### www.Daily-Debrief.com/Book-Bonus

# THE DAILY DEBRIEF
CHALLENGE

## WEEK 1

## THE DAILY DEBRIEF ASSESSMENT

On a scale of 1-10, with 1 being poor and 10 being excellent, how would you rate the following areas of your life?

Career and Business

Love and Romance

Finances

Faith and Spirituality

Health and Wellness

Fun and Recreation

Friends and Family

Contribution/Volunteering

Plot your scores on the High-Performance Life Wheel by placing a dot on the circle corresponding to your score.

**WEEK 1**                    **DATE:**   /   /

---------- **HIGH-PERFORMANCE LIFE WHEEL** ----------

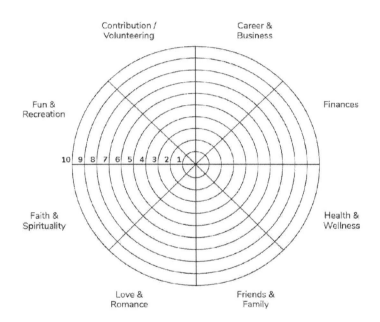

---------- **WEEKLY FOCUS AREA** ----------

This week I will improve

..................................................................................................
..................................................................................................
..................................................................................................

**WEEK 1, DAY 1**                    DATE:    /    /

―――――――――― **STEP 1 - GRATITUDE** ――――――――――

Three things I'm grateful for are

① .............................................................................................................
② .............................................................................................................
③ .............................................................................................................

―――――――――― **STEP 2 - REVIEW MY MISSION** ――――――――――

My mission is to ...................................................................................
............................................................................................................

―――――――――― **STEP 3 - EVALUATE TODAY** ――――――――――

1. Did I live my mission today?                ☐ Yes / ☐ No
2. What worked, and how do I repeat it?

① .............................................................................................................
② .............................................................................................................
③ .............................................................................................................

3. What didn't work, and how do I improve it?

① .............................................................................................................

―――――――――― **STEP 4 - ANTICIPATE TOMORROW** ――――――――――

**1. Identify Tomorrow's Daily 3**

▸ What are three simple, specific, and easily achievable tasks I can do to be better tomorrow?

① .............................................................................................................
② .............................................................................................................
③ .............................................................................................................

**2. Chair Fly Success**

▸ Visualize accomplishing each of tomorrow's Daily 3.

## STEP 5 - TIME FOR LESSONS LEARNED

What were today's lessons learned?

**WEEK 1, DAY 2**          **DATE:**    /    /

---------- **STEP 1 - GRATITUDE** ----------

Three things I'm grateful for are

① .................................................................................................................
② .................................................................................................................
③ .................................................................................................................

---------- **STEP 2 - REVIEW MY MISSION** ----------

My mission is to .........................................................................................
..........................................................................................................................

---------- **STEP 3 - EVALUATE TODAY** ----------

1. Did I live my mission today?                    ☐ Yes / ☐ No
2. What worked, and how do I repeat it?

① .................................................................................................................
② .................................................................................................................
③ .................................................................................................................

3. What didn't work, and how do I improve it?

① .................................................................................................................

---------- **STEP 4 - ANTICIPATE TOMORROW** ----------

**1. Identify Tomorrow's Daily 3**

▶ What are three simple, specific, and easily achievable tasks I can do to be better tomorrow?

① .................................................................................................................
② .................................................................................................................
③ .................................................................................................................

**2. Chair Fly Success**

▶ Visualize accomplishing each of tomorrow's Daily 3.

## STEP 5 - TIME FOR LESSONS LEARNED

What were today's lessons learned?

**WEEK 1, DAY 3**  DATE:   /   /

──────── **STEP 1 - GRATITUDE** ────────

Three things I'm grateful for are

1. ........................................................................................
2. ........................................................................................
3. ........................................................................................

──────── **STEP 2 - REVIEW MY MISSION** ────────

My mission is to ..................................................................
........................................................................................

──────── **STEP 3 - EVALUATE TODAY** ────────

1. Did I live my mission today?            ☐ Yes / ☐ No
2. What worked, and how do I repeat it?

1. ........................................................................................
2. ........................................................................................
3. ........................................................................................

3. What didn't work, and how do I improve it?

1. ........................................................................................

──────── **STEP 4 - ANTICIPATE TOMORROW** ────────

**1. Identify Tomorrow's Daily 3**

▸ What are three simple, specific, and easily achievable tasks I can do to be better tomorrow?

1. ........................................................................................
2. ........................................................................................
3. ........................................................................................

**2. Chair Fly Success**

▸ Visualize accomplishing each of tomorrow's Daily 3.

## STEP 5 - TIME FOR LESSONS LEARNED

What were today's lessons learned?

**WEEK 1, DAY 4**                    **DATE:**    /    /

──────────────── **STEP 1 - GRATITUDE** ────────────────

Three things I'm grateful for are

① ........................................................................................
② ........................................................................................
③ ........................................................................................

──────────────── **STEP 2 - REVIEW MY MISSION** ────────────────

My mission is to ....................................................................
........................................................................................

──────────────── **STEP 3 - EVALUATE TODAY** ────────────────

1. Did I live my mission today?                    ☐ Yes / ☐ No
2. What worked, and how do I repeat it?

① ........................................................................................
② ........................................................................................
③ ........................................................................................

3. What didn't work, and how do I improve it?

① ........................................................................................

──────────────── **STEP 4 - ANTICIPATE TOMORROW** ────────────────

**1. Identify Tomorrow's Daily 3**

▸ What are three simple, specific, and easily achievable tasks I can do to be better tomorrow?

① ........................................................................................
② ........................................................................................
③ ........................................................................................

**2. Chair Fly Success**

▸ Visualize accomplishing each of tomorrow's Daily 3.

## STEP 5 - TIME FOR LESSONS LEARNED

What were today's lessons learned?

**WEEK 1, DAY 5**  DATE:  /  /

---------- **STEP 1 - GRATITUDE** ----------

Three things I'm grateful for are

① ....................................................................................................................
② ....................................................................................................................
③ ....................................................................................................................

---------- **STEP 2 - REVIEW MY MISSION** ----------

My mission is to ..................................................................................................
................................................................................................................................

---------- **STEP 3 - EVALUATE TODAY** ----------

1. Did I live my mission today?                    ☐ Yes / ☐ No
2. What worked, and how do I repeat it?

① ....................................................................................................................
② ....................................................................................................................
③ ....................................................................................................................

3. What didn't work, and how do I improve it?

① ....................................................................................................................

---------- **STEP 4 - ANTICIPATE TOMORROW** ----------

1. **Identify Tomorrow's Daily 3**

   ▶ What are three simple, specific, and easily achievable tasks I can do to be better tomorrow?

① ....................................................................................................................
② ....................................................................................................................
③ ....................................................................................................................

2. **Chair Fly Success**

   ▶ Visualize accomplishing each of tomorrow's Daily 3.

## STEP 5 - TIME FOR LESSONS LEARNED

What were today's lessons learned?

**WEEK 1, DAY 6**  DATE:   /   /

---------- **STEP 1 - GRATITUDE** ----------

Three things I'm grateful for are

① .................................................................................
② .................................................................................
③ .................................................................................

---------- **STEP 2 - REVIEW MY MISSION** ----------

My mission is to ...............................................................
................................................................................

---------- **STEP 3 - EVALUATE TODAY** ----------

1. Did I live my mission today?         ☐ Yes / ☐ No
2. What worked, and how do I repeat it?

① .................................................................................
② .................................................................................
③ .................................................................................

3. What didn't work, and how do I improve it?

① .................................................................................

---------- **STEP 4 - ANTICIPATE TOMORROW** ----------

**1. Identify Tomorrow's Daily 3**

▶ What are three simple, specific, and easily achievable tasks I can do to be better tomorrow?

① .................................................................................
② .................................................................................
③ .................................................................................

**2. Chair Fly Success**

▶ Visualize accomplishing each of tomorrow's Daily 3.

## STEP 5 - TIME FOR LESSONS LEARNED

What were today's lessons learned?

**WEEK 1, DAY 7**  DATE:  /  /

──────────── **STEP 1 - GRATITUDE** ────────────

Three things I'm grateful for are

①...................................................................................................
②...................................................................................................
③...................................................................................................

──────────── **STEP 2 - REVIEW MY MISSION** ────────────

My mission is to ....................................................................................
...................................................................................................

──────────── **STEP 3 - EVALUATE TODAY** ────────────

1. Did I live my mission today?                  ☐ Yes / ☐ No
2. What worked, and how do I repeat it?

①...................................................................................................
②...................................................................................................
③...................................................................................................

3. What didn't work, and how do I improve it?

①...................................................................................................

──────────── **STEP 4 - ANTICIPATE TOMORROW** ────────────

**1. Identify Tomorrow's Daily 3**

▸ What are three simple, specific, and easily achievable tasks I can do to be better tomorrow?

①...................................................................................................
②...................................................................................................
③...................................................................................................

**2. Chair Fly Success**

▸ Visualize accomplishing each of tomorrow's Daily 3.

## STEP 5 - TIME FOR LESSONS LEARNED

What were today's lessons learned?

## About The Author

Jeff Bonner is a combat veteran who served as a fighter-attack pilot in Iraq and Afghanistan. He is an experienced military commander and a former Harvard National Security Fellow who shares the leadership principles that drive the high-performance world of military aviation.

Bagram Air Base, Afghanistan—Jeff "Bones" Bonner after returning from a combat mission in northern Afghanistan. Now it's time for the most important part of the mission—the debrief.

(Photo courtesy of the author)

Printed in Poland
by Amazon Fulfillment
Poland Sp. z o.o., Wrocław

29506224R00068